Until We Meet Again

K.D. Massi

Until We Meet Again. Copyright © by K.D. Massi.

All rights reserved. Printed in the United States of America.

No part of this book may be used or reproduced in any manner whatsoever without written permission except in the case of brief quotations embodied in critical articles and reviews.

For information, address DW Creative Publishers, 5 Cowboys Way; Frisco, TX 75034.

DW Creative Publishers books may be purchased for business, educational, religious, or sales promotional use.

For information, please email
connect@dwcreativepublishers.com.

FIRST EDITION

Cover design by: DW Creative Publishers

Interior design by: DW Creative Publishers

Editing by: DW Creative Publishers

PRINT BOOK: ISBN 978-1-952605-30-7

EBOOK: ISBN 978-1-952605-31-4

Library of Congress Control Number: 2023903614

For Jayden,

You will always be my favorite person, and the best thing in my life. I hope you always have the courage to speak your truth. I love you the most.

For Daddy,

Thank you for your unlimited sacrifices and love. Thank you for introducing me to my love of music. Most of all, thank you for being my hero.

For Traci,

I am forever blessed that you are my mother. And I am forever grateful that I had you as my gold standard. You are always with me, and I strive daily to follow your example.

For Mama,

Thank you for being there for the countless late night phone conversations and giving me encouragement.

For Demond,

I hope you catch all the messages from above, like you always did when you were here.

And for anyone who always felt the emotions and had the words to say, but they were stuck on your throat.

Try Again. Fail Again. Fail Better
Samuel Beckett

CONTENTS

IT'S ALL IN HOW YOU SAY IT 1
PART I: IM THANKFUL…I THINK 5
    THROUGH THE CLOUDS 12
    A FIELD OF STRAWBERRIES FOR TRACI 14
    REMINISCE 16
    4:01 (JAYDEN'S SONG) 18
    A BREATH OF FRESH AIR FOR DEMOND 21
PART II: THIS WILL ONLY HURT A LOT (RELATIONSHIPS) 23
    CRASH INTO YOU 31
    WITHOUT YOU 33
    ILLUSION 35
    DISMISS 36
    ALL OVER AGAIN 38
    SUDDENLY 41
    SHATTER 45
    YOU 47
    LINGERING 50
    HEALING 51
    ONE MORE TIME 53
    THE UNCHOSEN 55
    UNTIL WE MEET AGAIN 56
    WHAT ABOUT US 58
    I WROTE THIS SONG 60
    I'VE BEEN LOVING YOU SO LONG 64
    YOU'LL NEVER KNOW 65
    FADED 68

SUBCONSCIOUSLY	71
LETTING GO	72
BLIND	74
LOVE SONG	76
WRAPPED UP	79
PART III: THIS ISN'T EVEN MY BEST LOOK	**81**
IT'S OCTOBER, AGAIN	85
THE WAY CHRISTMAS SHOULD BE	89
HOW MANY MORE CHRISTMASES	91
WILL I (AGAIN)	95
FALL AWAY	97
INVISIBLE	99
PART IV: A MILLION SMALL STEPS	**103**
ISOLATION	108
ANYTHING	110
MY LIFE, SO FAR	114
A LITTLE CONTEXT BEHIND MY WORK	**117**

IT'S ALL IN HOW YOU SAY IT

For as long as I can remember, it's always been me, my pen, and my notebook of thoughts. I knew I wanted to be a writer as a child, because I would invent stories and songs as a way to be fun and creative.

I suppose I've always been a bit of a dreamer, and when I was younger my imagination was my best friend. As I got older, I became more fascinated with words. I loved reading books, newspapers, and magazine articles. This was before the age of the Internet.

I also loved music of all kinds. In fact, music has always been so healing for me. I recall being so moved by certain songs, and the way the artist would pull me in by telling a story with the lyrics. Other than singing in my room, I knew that it wouldn't be my profession. But writing has always stayed with me.

What I didn't realize back then was how so much of my experiences would set the stage for me to be so expressive. To say I've been through a lot would be a huge understatement. I know that no one is exempt from trials and tribulations in life, however it still doesn't stop the sting in the moment that it's happening. I believe that when you go through a lot, you end up having a lot to say.

We all have different perspectives, and we tell our stories based on our own perspectives, either good or bad. I wanted to share my story from the stance of someone who has been able to reflect fully on the aspects of her life without giving the perception that I am frozen in time. I wanted to be fully transparent with my feelings.

To do so, I had to invade every emotion whether it was happiness, heartbreak, grief, anger, confusion, confidence, or simply not giving a damn. I had to put it all out there. It was the only way I could truly give my heart a voice. Throughout my writing process, there were times when I was a little discouraged. I wondered if my experiences were valid enough that they would resonate with others. I also worried about whether my words would reach people in the way I intended. I obsessed over every scenario because, on one hand I wanted to be completely open. However, I also wanted to speak in a way that was respectful of myself as well as others.

Eventually, I allowed myself to reveal my heart unapologetically. There have been numerous times where I have swallowed my feelings, when I just wanted to scream them all out. I have held my tongue for the sake of peace during moments that I wanted to tell it all and be disruptive. Writing has always been the space where I could let it all go and do just that because the thoughts had to go somewhere. And I am so thankful that I have the ability to turn my thoughts into points of expression. I get to create and recreate various moments of my life and turn them into keepsakes.

Writing has constantly followed me around, like a never-ending shadow, even in those times where I was stuck and unable to properly articulate my words. When I couldn't fully focus on completing a piece, I would write things down in shorthand for the sake of notation. Then, when I was ready, and my mind was right I would finish.

Sometimes, the process took longer than I wanted or anticipated. There are a few songs and poems that initially started as a one or two sentence thought in my head. But I knew that I wouldn't be satisfied until the thought was translated. That may sound simple, but it can be internally frustrating when you have so much you want to let out, yet everything is swirling around in your head. It's like a double-edged sword because having a gift is amazing, however it can also drive you crazy.

The title of the book holds a double meaning. **Until We Meet Again** is a song I wrote about a past relationship (included in a later part of the book). However, the title also represents me and the many times I had to come back to myself. There were situations in my life where I felt I lost parts of me while trying to prove myself to other people in order to live up to their expectations. I can admit that I had to hit the same wall quite a bit before I realized that I could no longer afford to contribute to my own self-inflicted harm. I had to stand up for myself. I also had to learn to show up for myself. In doing so, I was reintroduced to a better version of who I am.

My purpose for writing this book was to give readers a glimpse into my life. My hope is that I can speak to others, while they learn about me through my songs, poems, personal stories, and sprinkles of what I like to call my own "wisdom nuggets" that I have learned to live by. These are my words, my struggles, my successes, my thoughts, and my feelings. The best part is that I get to convey it all through what I like to call an "artistic memoir" comprised of specific moments.

All of the time periods of my life are pieced together to tell the story of a woman who is still learning, healing and growing more everyday. I wanted to honor those periods of my life that affected me the most. I wanted to heal, let go, and move forward, while also reflecting on the memories that mean so much to me.

Regardless of the outcome, everything that has happened in my life has made me into the person that I am, and it continues to shape me today. So, this is for those who have felt overlooked, left out, misunderstood, or misjudged. It is dedicated to anyone who has ever felt lonely, broken, heartache, and a little rage. Yet even still, they have remained faithful and steadfast enough to turn the most bitter lemons into their own acquired taste of lemonade. You are me, and I am you.

PART I

IM THANKFUL…I THINK

I have so many great memories of my childhood; however, it was anything but normal. I am a true Texas girl. I was born in Dallas, and I have resided in the state all my life. I went to live with my father when I was 5, and I stayed with him until I was 21. I have always been in awe of my dad. Anytime I heard his voice, I knew I was safe, and I still feel that way today. He's not perfect, and he definitely made some mistakes (as we all do). But his love for me was always evident and visible. He is warm and kind, and he did his best to make sure I was happy even in the rough moments. I know without a doubt that I was his number one priority from the moment I went to live with him. He saved my life without hesitation, and for that he will always be my hero.

But even though I had my dad, my mother's absence played had a big effect on how I navigated through my life and my relationships. I love my mother more than she knows, and I know that she loves me. It took me a long time, but as I got older, I was able to forgive her for not raising me, and the many moments we missed out on as mother and daughter. We have a good relationship now, but I know that our relationship is not as strong as it would have been if she had been a constant presence in my life. I realize her not being there caused an emptiness inside that has always lingered. It also caused me to feel that I wasn't important at a young age, and that feeling consequently was a reoccurring emotion throughout my life. I realize that she had her own demons that she had to fight, but as a child you don't understand.

All you see and know is that your parent is not around, and internally you think it's your fault. So of course, I thought she left because of me. I come from a very large family; however, I have always been the closest with the family on my mother's side. To this day, we are all extremely close.

Collectively, we are quite an interesting bunch. We have our moments, but we love hard, we fight for each other hard, and we enjoy each other so much.

Here's a fun backstory: My mom and two of her sisters were pregnant at the same time. It blew our grandparents away! My grandfather used to joke that they were trying to get him to start a nursery business. We were all born in 1982. My cousin, Deraund was born September 27, 1982, my cousin, Brandon was born December 6, 1982, and I was born exactly a week later on December 13, 1982. Close doesn't even begin to describe us. They have always been more like brothers than cousins to me. We will fight to the end for each other and we actually have a few times.

Unfortunately, loss has also been a constant in all our lives, and my earliest remembrance of tough loss was in 1992. My grandmother was diagnosed with uterine cancer, and she fought a hard battle with the illness. As her condition deteriorated, we knew that we wanted to spend as much time with her as possible. Because of that, I spent Thanksgiving of '92 with my mother's family. I remember playing with my cousins, and we were having a great time when my grandfather came to tell us that our grandmother had passed away in the house. Just like that.

When you are 9, you can't fully process what death means, but I knew it meant that she would no longer be with us, and that was an awful feeling. I also remember thinking that this is not what Thanksgiving is supposed to be. I was expecting a day of happiness, and fellowship, not grief. By far the worst part was seeing my mom and my aunt's faces. I recall them trying to be so strong for us kids, but I could look at them and tell that they were broken. For a long time after, that was my memory of Thanksgiving. I always equated the day with death, and it was just a really bad holiday to me.

My dad met my stepmother, Traci, when I was 7. From the moment she came into my life, she was amazing. It was through her that I learned that you don't have to be blood to have an unbreakable bond with someone, and for them to be family. She was, and she will always be my mother. She was patient, and smart, and tough, and loving, and funny and beautiful. There are not enough adjectives I could use to describe her. But one of the things that stood out about her was that she was unafraid and unapologetic with how she lived her life and the decisions she made. Don't get me wrong, she was also very headstrong, and we also had some intense disagreements, especially as I entered my teen years. When her and my dad were married, I remember feeling like I finally had a complete family. And we had some great moments with just the three of us.

When I was in middle school, Traci was diagnosed with breast cancer. I remember being so scared, especially considering the previous losses in my family from some form of the disease. I immediately thought of my grandmother, and the way she had passed, and I worried that my mother would suffer the same fate. It wasn't easy, but she completed all of her treatments and went into remission. She was feeling good, so I thought everything would be smooth from that point. When I was in 10 grade, her cancer returned and this time it was much more aggressive. It spread to other parts of her body, and it caused her to deteriorate quickly. She died on July 16, 1999.

Initially, when things started to go downhill, the report that we received from the doctor was that she had six months to live. That was just unfathomable to me. I couldn't think of how I could cram so many quality moments into such a short period of time. I remember talking to my mom, and in my mind, I was trying to will her to live. Up until that moment, I didn't understand the severity of her condition because she was always so strong. She never let on that she was suffering in any way.

There were so many things that I wanted her to be here for including my high school prom and graduation, my wedding, seeing her first grandchild, and just life in general. I knew she was fighting, and she was tired, but I also knew she was trying to hold on. When I brought up my graduation, she told me that she would be there, even if it was in a wheelchair. I told her I loved her, and we hung up the phone. She died a week later. Exactly six months after she was rediagnosed.

I knew when the phone rang the morning she died that she was gone before the words were even said. But even after my dad told me, it's like time stopped. I literally had an out of body experience because I felt that pieces of my heart were leaving me. It just didn't make any sense. I don't know how I made it through the days and months after that because everything was a blur.

I was literally numb on the day of her funeral. I remembered how broken my mom and aunts were when my grandmother died, and I immediately understood the pain. I remember walking into the church, and seeing her casket, and hearing "When the Saints Go Marching In" playing on instrumental. To this day, I can't stand to hear that song. My junior year of high school was awful because I was in so much pain. I would listen to how everyone around me was so excited for all the things we had coming up as upper class men. But all I could think was that my mother was gone, and my happiness had left with her. I was raised as a Christian; however, I was so angry at God for allowing my mother to be taken. We are taught to believe that everything happens for a bigger reason, but I couldn't comprehend any of that at the time. I couldn't find the purpose of her death. I didn't feel that my mother's passing did anything but cause pain to everyone that loved her, and I was just so mad.

Looking back to that time, I know that I should have had grief counseling after my mother's death because I really had no clue on how to deal with the weight of it all. Grief is a constant ache. It literally stops you in your tracks and it takes your breath away. Thinking from one moment to the next is almost impossible. The pain is like quicksand. It surrounds your heart, and it doesn't let up with pulling you under.

When my mom passed away, my dad continued to work his night shifts at the bank. So, I was alone until the morning when he came home to take me to school. Those nights alone were pure hell. I was so used to having my mom there, and for everything to be so silent and still was like a nightmare. In normal circumstances, being alone at night as a teenager would seem like the best thing ever. But it was actually the opposite.

Technically, I was 16 and old enough to take care of myself, but it was an adjustment, especially after a traumatic event. I remember many sleepless, tear filled nights where I just waited to join my mom. Since my grief had nowhere to go, I felt like I was dying. But no one knew how bad I was hurting because I didn't tell them. There were so many people in pain over my mother's death, and I felt that sharing my pain would overwhelm them even more. My dad was falling apart. The relationship between him and my mom had imploded in the months leading up to her death. I believe that they truly loved each other, but I don't think that either of them was the best at showing it.

I know that my dad carried the guilt of her final months on his shoulders, and I didn't want to burden him with my pain. Ironically, the first major holiday after my mother passed was Thanksgiving. It was just as awful as the Thanksgiving that my grandmother passed away seven years prior. I don't remember smiling, or enjoying family time, or even the taste of food. I just remember feeling empty, and everything around me was so surreal.

You never stop missing your loved ones once they are no longer here. The ache is always there, but time does help to lessen the severity. There was a time where I never felt I would be okay. But I can say that I have had many wonderful Thanksgivings since 1999 with my amazing family, and all holidays got especially better once my son was born.

Even though my time with my mother was very short, it was memorable. I don't always talk about her because it's still hard being without her even after 21 years. But I'm so thankful that she was part of my life. The unconditional love that she gave me helped me to be a parent later in life, and a better woman in general.

WISDOM NUGGET 1

There's nothing more therapeutic than allowing every emotion to ripple through your heart and spill onto a page.

THROUGH THE CLOUDS

Even though I'm grown I can't believe
I'm doing life without you here
Because in my worst case scenario
I never pictured a reality where you weren't near
So many years have come and gone
Yet still a large part of me is so empty
I'll never be able to erase the feeling of the day
My whole life changed at the age of sixteen

Left wondering how
I'm supposed to go on now
Without the comfort of your touch
And the certainty of your love

It hurts that you're not
Physically here with me now
But I can always look up and feel your love
Radiating through the clouds
It's my confirmation
That you're never far
And I know that you're guiding me
From wherever you are

I suppose the truth is that I felt you leaving
But I didn't get the chance to say goodbye
I was so in denial
And I'll never fully understand why
Losing you was devastating

My sorrow was so deep
And for so many years I inadvertently
Blocked it from my memory

Left wondering how
I'm supposed to go on now
Without the comfort of your touch
And the certainty of your love

It hurts that you're not
Physically here with me now
But I can always look up and feel your love
Radiating through the clouds
It's my confirmation
That you're never far
And I know that you're guiding me
From wherever you are

Although my world will never be the same
I try to be a reflection of the life you lived
And when I'm missing our conversations
I like to visualize the advice you'd give
I'd give anything just to see your face
But I know you've elevated
To a better place
And no matter what I go through
I can always look to the sky
To connect to you

A FIELD OF STRAWBERRIES FOR TRACI

I haven't forgotten anything about you
All of the moments stay with me
I can still picture every detail about you
It's all permanently reserved in my memory
From the genuine warmth of your smile
And the radiance of your skin
If I close my eyes I can distinctly smell
The fragrance of your favorite scent
I still hear your voice vibrating so clearly
The echoes of your laughter I'll always carry
And even though you've been gone for so long
I know we'll meet again one day in a field of strawberries

WISDOM NUGGET 2

I've been through so much in my life. I've had my fair share of pain, and quite a bit of struggles. There were many times where I would think, "why me?" The bright spot about the hard times has been my writing. For me, writing is a way to release and connect with others who may be able to relate.

REMINISCE

Sometimes I sit and think about the way
The carefree way we lived life back in the day
Vivid conversations of talking tough with my best friends
Staying up late to meet the sunrise every weekend
Remembering how we would roam around the neighborhood
happy to be on our own
Staying away until the lightening bugs called us home
Counting down the years until we turned eighteen
Clueless about what adult life would truly mean

Those days are far gone
And I admit that they are missed
But it's always a good and mellow vibe for me
To sit back and reminisce
Thinking about those sacred moments
And how incredible they used to be
I know I can't go back
So I keep everything stored inside of my mentally nostalgic diary

Every now and then I think back to the times
When love was fresh and new to my heart and mind
Rushing to get home and talk on the telephone
Flirting while the background played our favorite R&B song
I recall those long handwritten letters to express our feelings
Detailing everything we were concealing
Break and make-ups was all we'd do
Flashbacks of 422 with you and you (and yeah you too)

Those days are far gone
And I admit that they are missed
But it's always a good and mellow vibe for me
To sit back and reminisce
Thinking about those sacred moments
And how incredible they used to be
I know I can't go back
So I keep everything stored inside of my mentally nostalgic diary

I'm so grateful for the days we were so inseparable
Even if I know our paths detaching was inevitable
And although I
Sometimes ache for the days passed by
The lasting evocations of us make it alright
You will always be an irreplaceable part of my life

4:01 (JAYDEN'S SONG)

Long before you came to be
I wished for you
To the point that when you were real
I didn't believe that it was true
As I sat in the waiting room
I silently said a prayer
For God's grace to cover you
If in fact you were actually there
And when I received the confirmation
Every feeling and instinct kicked in
Without any hesitation

And you are the best part of me
I'm forever the lucky one
Nothing on earth compares to the bond
Between a mother and her son
The love I have for you is like no other
You will always be second to none
Because everything in my life changed completely
On September seventeenth at 4:01

Watching you grow into a young man
Is so surreal because you're no longer my little boy
But every stage and moment is such a pleasure
You bring me everlasting joy
When I look into your face
I realize my purpose so clearly
Because your presence is proof

That this life wasn't discouraged of me
So take my hand and let's conquer the world together
No matter how far you go
We are attached at the heart forever

And you are the best part of me
I'm forever the lucky one
Nothing on earth compares to the bond
Between a mother and her son
The love I have for you is like no other
You will always be second to none
Because everything in my life changed completely
On September seventeenth at 4:01

You'll always be my heartbeat
And there are times I'm still taking it all in
But I know my definition of blessed
Is spelled J-A-Y-D-E-N

LOSS

When someone leaves suddenly there is no time to prepare. There's no time to react. And you miss the chance to have that one last time.

A BREATH OF FRESH AIR FOR DEMOND

I didn't expect you to leave so suddenly
I'm sitting here wondering how can this be
When you were here everything was bright
Now you're gone and it's all so empty
I thought that you would be here
To witness it all
You'd catch all the subliminal subtleties
When I expressed it all
And I realize that I
Can't tell you face to face
But I know that you can hear me
Whenever I talk to you from that sacred place
I'm so thankful for connection between us
All of the things we didn't have to say
And it hurts that I can no longer see you
Because you've floated away
Even though now the days feel different
I know you are never far
Because anytime I am missing you
My heart can reach you wherever you are
Every time I close my eyes
I hope you know
My soul is instantly attached to you
I sense your glow
And I am filled with tranquility
Your spirit surrounds me running free
Because I feel your never ending love
Wrapped around me

And I hope it shows
That it was always a pleasure
To give you unconditional love
And I will always treasure
The many souvenirs left
Of every moment spent with you
And you will forever be
The one that I belong to

PART II

THIS WILL ONLY HURT A LOT (RELATIONSHIPS)

I honestly don't think there are enough words or pages for me to speak about my relationship experiences. But I suppose I can give a condensed cliffs notes version. I started dating at seventeen (I've always considered myself to be a late bloomer with everything). Throughout my life, I have loved four men. Every experience was different, but they were all memorable in their own way.

One was what I like to call my kindred spirit, however I feel that we were met with bad timing more than once. To this day, he is one of my favorite people. I used to consider him to be my soulmate. Over time, I realized the meaning of the word was not reduced to love. A lot of people think a soulmate is the person you ultimately end up with, however that's not always the case.

A soulmate can as intimate as a lover, or as innocent as a friend (among other things). For me, it was the natural flow of the connection, and the unforced chemistry between he and I that was so unmatched. There's nothing like being able to laugh and be silly with someone one moment, then switching into a serious no holds barred conversation the next. It's amazing how you can both be so in sync, yet you know that you have to part to grow. It wasn't easy to accept this, but it was necessary. If I am honest with myself, I know that one of the reasons everything was so easy with us was because the relationship never got too deep. But, whenever I was with him, the moments (however brief) were just…everything.

With another, the relationship was everything you dream of and fear at the same time. We were 18 when we met, but for me it was the best of times. Still, in the beginning, we were both too young and immature to build a relationship on a serious level in a way that would have been of substance. When you are young, you don't know how to handle what you haven't experienced. You are learning as you go. So of course, the first go round is the most amazing, imperfect, wonderful, horrible, intense, dramatic experience you can have. At least it was for me! The range of emotions I felt during this time was out of control. Have you ever had to work a retail job in the mall while dealing with heartbreak? It's torture!

First loves are not always meant to last. But this relationship was the beginning of a heart that was figuring out how to love and be loved. For that reason, it will always be memorable. I remember every detail of our history that spanned 20 years. At first, it was hard to navigate around one another. However, as we got older, we reached a place where we were able to be good friends that could have a conversation about the past, present, and future (and everything in between).

We were able to be understanding of where we were in our lives, and respectful of our boundaries. Because we were living our lives, we would sometimes go long periods of time without speaking. But when we would reconnect, it was as if no time were lost. As long as I knew he wasn't far and that he was okay, I was okay. Our connection was one that that could not be explained, and I never wanted to. It just was. It was with him that I learned what it meant to love someone unconditionally, without a thought. When you genuinely love someone, you learn that sometimes the best thing for you both is that you are not together even when it's what that you want more than anything. That was our story. And through it all, I loved him from the day I met him at 18, until the day he departed this life. And I will love him until I leave this life, and after.

The next was a 13-year relationship that honestly ran its course long before we officially ended things. We experienced so much together and were engaged a couple of times. Although it never led to marriage, a lot transpired throughout the duration of our time together. After all, 13 years is longer than some marriages last. Wanting to be right about something and wanting to say, "I win" can cause us to linger longer in things than we should. And the issue with lingering is that you can't fully grow the way that you need to. As a result, you hold on to comfort and convenience, rather than what's real.

Over time, we became so familiar with each other than I began to look at him as more of the knight in shining armor. That may sound superficial, but that was his role with so many people in his life. I didn't like it, but after a while it became second nature for me to expect him to be the same way with me. I don't want to gloss over our relationship as though it was meaningless and superficial, because at one point I did think that we were going to spend the rest of our lives together. He is a great guy, and he meant so much to me for so long. It was a very real relationship that had a lot of love. But as a couple, I also experienced a lot of pain from someone who I trusted and who was supposed to be my partner. And it wasn't the kind of love that you would expect from such a long-term relationship.

Our son was the best thing that we did together, and his father and I are so committed to making sure he has a great life. He is definitely the best part of my life, and I could not have asked for a better child. There is truly no one like him! And even though my relationship with his father did not work out, he is the best thing to come out of our union.

And for that, I will always be grateful. I think some the best advantages that we can give to our children are love, laughter, stability, security, wisdom and strength regardless of the household size. I have had some challenging moments as a parent (and I am sure I will have more). But I truly feel that my son and I have such a great household that is full of warmth and free of stress. For now, it's the best thing for us, and I will forever be grateful that he was conceived in love.

And finally, there was the guy who was once strictly a friend who over time became so much more. Who doesn't love the story of the two friends that eventually fall in love! It's very I but l do believe love that starts as friendship can be a wonderful thing. When we met, I never thought we would become as close as we did. In fact, I wasn't sure if I even liked him as a person! But somehow, we would always end up in the same place at the same time. As we got to know each other I realized how amazing he was. We have so many similarities, but we are also quite different! So, bringing that together, and bridging the gap could be challenging at times.

The transition from friendship to relationship can be a great thing if both people are on the same page with what they want. It's not a decision that should be jumped into lightly, and you certainly must give the relationship the same amount of attention as you would give to someone that you've just met with no prior knowledge. I feel that we were great as friends, however my expectations of how I want to be treated are the same with everyone regardless of our history. And that's one of the ways it went left.

Oftentimes, we expect people to be accepting of who we are, to the point that we don't consider them the way we should. There were times that I wondered if we should have crossed the friendship and relationship line. When I think about if it was worth it, my answer is 100 percent yes. We have seen each other through every stage of life, through the best and the worst of times (and ourselves). With him, there is an unbreakable bond, an unspoken trust, and an unwavering love that will always be present.

I have had some unforgettable moments in love, and I have had other moments that I wish I could forget. Can I pinpoint where things went wrong in my relationships? In some ways, yes. There are numerous reasons, but the main ones for me personally were lack of communication and respect, dishonesty, and not being fully committed to building together. I don't ever claim to be perfect, but it can never be said that I am not completely transparent and honest about my feelings. I've always felt that it's imperative to tell people the things we want (and need) to say when the opportunity is there.

If you can't effectively communicate, it automatically puts your relationship at a disadvantage; it also opens the door for so many distractions to come in. And dishonesty has multiple connotations. It's not just infidelity, but it's also not being true to who you are, and what you want. In addition, it's not being forthcoming about how you really feel about your partner, and if they have a permanent place in your life. It's not always easy to have open conversations with someone, especially if you are telling them what they don't want to hear. Even still, the best thing you can do for someone you care about is to spare them precious time that they can't get back, and heartache that can take years to heal from.

When you experience abandonment at an earlier age, it can affect you mentally more than you know. I had one mother who was still physically present, however she wasn't a full time presence in my life. And my other mother died when I was at my most vulnerable. So, I was fighting a lot of negative thoughts. I never felt that I was worthy, and I always felt like people were being dishonest with me. And I always prepared myself for people to leave, because all I had to go by were the previous events in my life. So, how did all of that mix in with my relationships. Well, I was dealing with grief, trust, and abandonment issues. Not to mention my personal insecurities. Mix that in with guys who were also dealing with their own stuff and it's a recipe for combustion. So, you can imagine how fun it all was. (Insert sarcasm). I admit that I projected my own insecurities and shortcomings into a couple of my relationships because I didn't know how to completely deal, and they were affected. That is an area that I had to mature in and work on, even outside of my intimate relationships. Insecurity can be tricky because you struggle to trust your instincts, and if you are tied to someone who doesn't have your best interest in mind, they can try to use it against you. Me being aware of my shortfalls didn't make me oblivious to foolishness. In fact, my intuitions were spot on more than they were wrong when I felt that there was shadiness happening behind my back. This was also true in my friendships as well. After all, friendships are relationships too. Our friendships are precious because we tend to form them at a young age, and we want to carry them into each phase in our lives. We often learn that some friendships we outgrow, and some are one sided. Some hit a breaking point of no return. And some people, we realize that we weren't as close to them as we used to be (or we thought we were). I've went through every example, and none of it was easy. It's a hard line to walk when you have people in your life that you don't want to lose. Yet the effort to maintain the relationships is not reciprocated. So, I had to make the decisions to cut it off and let go. All of it hurt. It always hurts to when you have to let go of people that mean the world to you. I've always been a small circle type of person. I know that the people who were meant to be in my life for the long run still are.

I have loved hard in all my relationships, but I have also hurt deeply. And I am still grateful for every one. Was I misunderstood at times? Yes. Did things happen that were unfair? Absolutely. Did I make my fair share of blunders, and contribute to the breakdown of certain relationships? Without question. More than anything, I had to learn to forgive myself for not recognizing my value sooner. I had to forgive myself for holding on to people too tight, and for too long. And finally,

I had to acknowledge that it's okay to for me to move forward without certain people in my life, and it was okay for them to move forward without me in theirs.

WISDOM NUGGET 3

Real, true unconditional love ripples through your body, and radiates the spirit. So much so that being separated from the one you love causes a physical ache.

CRASH INTO YOU

It's been so long and I'm trying
Really trying to be strong and hold on
But deep inside I realize
That the time has come for me to move on
Golden pictures in the distance
Reminiscing on what we used to be
Teardrops are steady falling
It's so hard to accept that you and I are a memory

You are the love of my life
So much longing pain and sacrifice
All connected to you
Now it's over and still I'm

Steady moving forward
But I'm retracing my tracks
Head facing front and center
Still I turn and look back
Now everything is said and done
We're no longer, it's through
Still I look forward to the day
When I crash into you

No one can replace what you mean to me
And who you are in my heart
You were there
Affecting me from the start
To walk away means letting go of the hope

That you and I are meant to be
My heart is breaking inside
And I wish that you could see

You are the love of my life
So much longing pain and sacrifice
All connected to you
Now it's over and still I'm

Steady moving forward
But I'm retracing my tracks
Head facing front and center
Still I turn and look back
Now everything is said and done
We're no longer, it's through
Still I look forward to the day
When I crash into you

I'll never be able to escape
The love I have inside for you
Because in my heart I know
Our love will always be true
And at times it seems
That I see your face everywhere
I still hope one day when I turn around
You'll be standing there

WITHOUT YOU

I always believed together
You and I would be
Inevitably forever in each other's arms
Those days are a memory
Because now you're gone
And you can't see
Without you here
My soul is incomplete

To make things work
For us I've truly tried
Still pictures slowly fade
Of you and I

Never thought I's see a time
When your heart would drift
Away from mine
And I would have to grapple with letting go
Happiness replaced by sorrow
Emptiness inside soon follows
To move on hurts because you're all I know

I used to be convinced
That you and me
We ultimately destined
To be
Just when I thought the bond we shared ran deep
You turned and walked away

So easily

It feels like love is now a dying ember
As reflections start to wither
Leaving shadows of you and I
Laughter disappears into the wind
A broken heart is left to mend
Unsure if it will ever
Love that strong again

ILLUSION

Emotions are high
My strength is low
And right now
I'm unsure of the way to go
I wish I could look into your soul
And see your heart's true feelings
Because words only cause confusion
There are times that I feel like you're the one for me
Other times it's like we're just an illusion

DISMISS

I tried to do everything that I could do
To stay by your side because I was crazy about you
I begged, I pleaded
For your love, I needed
To feel your touch
Had to have you here
Felt my mind was gone without you near
But all the time that I was spending stressing over you
You were out there proving how much your love wasn't true
Your lying, your cheating
The mind games, deceiving
Got the best of me
I didn't wanna believe
But now I see we'll never be

Now there's nothing left to say
It's time for us to dismiss
One final goodbye
This is our last kiss
I have no more tears to cry
Baby I hate it's come down to this
But the love is fading
Perhaps in time, we'll look back and reminisce
But for now I'm letting go, I can't take no more
It's time for us to dismiss

Maybe it was all the sweet talk you fed to me

Or maybe it was the way my body trembled when you'd touch me softly
Thought that we were meant to be
Love had me blind, I couldn't see
Through all your lies
Thought you were true
You played with me, I was your fool
Now it's over and there's no more going back to you
Please believe I'm done with the heartache and there's nothing you can do
It hurts that our love is ending
But we can't go on pretending
My eyes are open wide to see
That you are not the one for me

Now there's nothing left to say
It's time for us to dismiss
One final goodbye
This is our last kiss
I have no more tears to cry
Baby I hate it's come down to this
But the love is fading
Perhaps in time, we'll look back and reminisce
But for now I'm letting go, I can't take no more
It's time for us to dismiss

You know that you really messed up this time
I always hold it in, but today I'm gonna speak my mind
Doesn't matter what you say
I'm still walking away
And deep down, you know it's true
That you'll never find another who can replicate my love for you

ALL OVER AGAIN

It's unexplainable
How you make me feel inside
So indescribable
That love has stood the test of time
So many years gone by
Yet here we are standing face to face
Passion strongly revived
All the memories have never been erased

And it's hard to deny the feelings
As I look into your eyes
It's so crazy to believe that after everything
Somehow you and I
Are still so intertwined
In a love that flows so high
Don't wanna let this get away
Can't we give us one more try

Baby please don't say
That we're not meant to be
When you know my heart
Is wrapped in you
And your love is all I need
Don't be so quick to turn away
From what you feel within
Because every time you come around
And then you leave
I have to heal all over again

You live in my heart
And you have captivated my soul
So I wanna hold on to this love
With you
I just can't let go
And I know
That you're calling out for me
We can't hide
What runs inside so deep

And it's hard to deny the feelings
As I look into your eyes
Lost love strongly revived
And now I realize
All that you are to me
And everything
That we can be
There's nothing better than you and I
I wanna know
Can't we give us one more try

Baby please don't say
That we're not meant to be
When you know my heart
Is wrapped in you
And your love is all I need
Don't be so quick to turn away
From what you feel within
Because every time you come around
And then you leave
I have to heal all over again

Won't you take the time
To look around and see

How much my heart beats just for you
Can't you see
I'm reaching for you
And there will never be
Any other romance
That comes close to you and me
I don't wanna say goodbye
So let's put our hearts together
And do love right this time

SUDDENLY

There you were
Standing right in front of me
But I was lost and caught up in a state
Of heartache and misery
I knew I wanted you
But I was too afraid to let my feelings get deep
But the more I tried to fight it
The harder it was to deny it
And I don't know when it happened, but

Suddenly you're here
And I can't believe my eyes
Holding me in your arms
Your lips meeting with mine
Just the thought of you
Sends shivers up my spine
I know I'm awake because
I've pinched myself a thousand times

Heard your footsteps
Coming up behind me
But I quickly ran away
I thought you were an illusion
And this feeling wouldn't stay
I tried to deny you
And overlook the truth
But your force was strong
You proved all my senses wrong

Don't know when it happened, but

Suddenly you're here
And I can't believe my eyes
Holding me in your arms
Your lips meeting with mine
Just the thought of you
Sends shivers up my spine
I know I'm awake because
I've pinched myself a thousand times

Never that that there would be
The possibility
That you would come along
And open my heart to so many amazing feelings
Had the blinders on my eyes
But somehow you dimmed the light
My lonely days are gone
With you nothing is wrong
Because you make everything alright

WISDOM NUGGET 4

Every detail of my life is vividly etched in my mind whether I like it or not.

WISDOM NUGGET 5

We often look to what's behind us for validation that we don't really need. Healing is followed by hard truths. For me that hard truth was the realization that my relationships were hitting a wall, not because of how I viewed others, but because of how they viewed me.

SHATTER

Are you really saying these words
Am I truly hearing you right
Because up until this moment it seemed
Like I was your world, and your light
But now you're telling me
It's not right
And we're no longer meant to be
I don't understand the sudden change
Can you sit down and talk to me
Is there anything I can say
If there's a chance to make it right
We've got to find a way

If we're done and it's over
My heart will shatter
There's no way I can just walk away
Leave it all behind
And pretend we never mattered
So please
Don't turn your back
And leave our love in the dust
This can't really be
The end of us
Because if it is
Then my whole heart will shatter

2 hours later and I'm still struggling
To pick myself up off the floor

It's hard to breathe, and my heart is in pieces
After watching you walk out my door
I don't wanna bear it
Are we really through
I'm guess I never fully realized
How much my heart was tied to you
Without you, everything is so bleak
I can't deny that if you're not here
It all means nothing
Do you feel anything at all
Or was it only me

If we're done and it's over
My heart will shatter
There's no way I can just walk away
Leave it all behind
And pretend we never mattered
So please
Don't turn your back
And leave our love in the dust
This can't really be
The end of us
Because if it is
Then my whole heart will shatter

If it's that easy for you to let go of me
And I'm wrong
Then my heart has misread everything
How can this be
That I was so intoxicated by you
I didn't realize
That love could be this cruel

YOU

When it's done, it's over
When it's over, it can't be saved
We tried so hard to keep us alive
But baby, we're slipping away
Still, it's so hard to walk away from love
And disregard my heart
Although it's all difficult to let go of
I gotta say

That you
Meant the world to me
And our love
Was everything
To me, and we
Were special baby
It was so amazing
So I had to let you know
It's been a fight
To let you go
I can only speak my truth
There will never be another one for me
Because that one is you

Reflecting my memories
My thoughts drift back to the times
When I was yours
And you were mine
We were so incredible

And those days
Were unforgettable
It's now out of my hands
Still, I gotta say

That you
Meant the world to me
And our love
Was everything
To me, and we
Were special baby
It was so amazing
So I had to let you know
It's been a fight
To let you go
I can only speak my truth
There will never be another one for me
Because that one is you

I can't comprehend
And I'll never know
Why we find love
Then have to let go
And I'm not sure
What else I can do
But I know for me
The one is always you

WISDOM NUGGET 6

Let the pain guide you to wisdom. Allow your experiences to be a steppingstone, so that your growth can direct you to those who truly understand your spirit.

LINGERING

This feels so evanescence
So lost in acquiescence
Ever since adolescence
I've been wrapped up in your presence
Please tell me how to feel
How am I supposed to deal
I'm so caught up in love's dust
Can't seem to untangle from us
No matter how hard I try
And I guess I'm steady concealing
It's a long process to healing
Because no matter what I do
I can't escape thoughts of me and you
My mind is always triggering
What's in my heart lingering

HEALING

It's 1 am
And I can't sleep
Every time I close my eyes
I see glimpses of you and me
So clearly in my mind
Thoughts running deep
You're always in my brain
Embedded in memory
Constantly flashing back
To those amazing times
When true love persevered
And your heart was mine

And its crazy how things can change
One moment everything is certain
The next it's all so estranged
(What I am supposed to do)
My heart is so worn out
Love you without any doubts
But you're nowhere around
I guess I'm forced to

So many days crying
My mind's gone and I'm reeling
Searching to understand
The pain I'm feeling
Countless nights spent wide awake
Thoughts are revealing

Slowly moving through the storm
To get to the healing

It's 2 am
I don't know what to do
Everything replaying back
Of us on continuous loop
So many thoughts swirling
Inside my head
I really believed in you
Every time you said
It would always be us together
Forever you and me
But I didn't realize that our love
Would fade to only temporary

And its crazy how things can change
One moment everything is certain
The next it's all so estranged
(What I am supposed to do)
My heart is so worn out
Love you without any doubts
But you're nowhere around
Emotions reduced to

So many days crying
My mind's gone and I'm reeling
Searching to understand
The pain I'm feeling
Countless nights spent wide awake
Thoughts are revealing
Slowly moving through the storm
To get to the healing

ONE MORE TIME

It seems to be a never-ending cycle
Of back and forth with you and me
Love hard, fight hard, make up, reconnect
Then we lather rinse repeat
And as much as we try
It's never quite enough
So I think this is goodbye
If only it were that easy

Because as much as I talk and I try
We both the pull is strong
And it's so hard to deny
My heart burns for you still
Love you and I always will
And I can't seem to let go, so

Before I close the door
I'm gonna try talking to you
One more time
Before we decide that we are completely done with each other
I'm communicating everything that's on my mind
When it comes down to you there's no ego
I'll always swallow my pride
And I've learned to never say never
Because with you it's always one more time

It's hard to imagine
You and me

Far apart without each other
Our love engulfed in memory
So I've endured the pain
Cried countless tears
And I've walked through the rain
But now something has gotta give

Because as much as I talk and I try
We both the pull is strong
And it's so hard to deny
My heart burns for you still
Love you and I always will
And I can't seem to let go, so

Before I close the door
I'm gonna try talking to you
One more time
Before we decide that we are completely done with each other
I'm communicating everything that's on my mind
When it comes down to you there's no ego
I'll always swallow my pride
And I've learned to never say never
Because with you it's always one more time

There's so much more
I want to say
And I wonder do you have it in you
To meet me halfway
If you just tell me what you need
Without hesitation
I know that we can be
Everything to one another in love

THE UNCHOSEN

I am the girl who believed in love
With white picket fences
Even though you were the curious guy
Who wanted to sow your oats with many others
I am the young woman who stayed loyal
Even though she experienced pain and heartbreak
While you were the guy who wanted the benefits
Of a relationship without the commitment
I am the one who believed in the purity
And the natural chemistry of our connection
Yet, you were the one who couldn't see yourself
Settling into a life with another out of fear of another failed relationship
I am the woman who truly felt
That you would have her best interest at heart
While you were the guy who was uncompromising
And all about self
I am the one who went through the toughest storms
Only to make it easier for the next one to experience the rainbow
I am the woman who has been waiting for you to see her fully
But you are the guy too full of blinders
To be completely present
So who am I
I am the unchosen

UNTIL WE MEET AGAIN

I remember that cold January night
When you and me
Came together and added another recollection
To our history
As we sat and talked under the moonlight
About nothing and everything
The simplicity of it all
Is one of my favorite memories
I was so caught up in your presence
And I just
Wanted our connection to last forever

And in that moment you were mine
And I was your only
I was able to be vulnerable
And my heart didn't feel so lonely
The ability to be free and let go
Longing so subdued that it was hard to hold it in
Those moments are only reserved for you
I'll hold them close until we meet again

I still remember that night
And every word you said to me
The experience was fleeting
But we made it feel like eternity
As we rushed hand in hand
To escape out of the winter breeze
I was so captivated

Then you pulled me closer to you gently
So mesmerized and full of bliss
I still get butterflies
When I recall every kiss

And in that moment you were mine
And I was your only
I was able to be vulnerable
And my heart didn't feel so lonely
The ability to be free and let go
Longing so subdued that it was hard to hold it in
Those moments are only reserved for you
I'll hold them close until we meet again

And although it's a little bittersweet
I know that we will
Always live on endlessly
I'll keep the memory of you and I
Tucked deep within
And my heart will wait patiently
Until we meet again

WHAT ABOUT US

What if I told you
That I let my thoughts get the best of me
To the point that I couldn't trust
And what if I said that I realize
We ended so abruptly because I didn't have faith in us
And I can't believe I had you here with me
But there was so much more to you
That I couldn't see
I'm standing here now
Hoping that we haven't lost it all

Because sometimes even with the best intentions
We incidentally hurt the ones that ride for us
I admit I messed up
But I don't want it to be over so suddenly
It should be you and me together
Can we take the time to discuss
What about us

Not having you here
Has left me so affected
Without you near my heart
Feels so neglected
And I know everything is all on me
I can't take the pain
Of being without your love
I don't know
What the hell I was thinking of

But now I recognize
How much it means
To have you in my life

Because sometimes even with the best intentions
We incidentally hurt the ones that ride for us
I admit I messed up
But I don't want it to be over so suddenly
It should be you and me together
Can we take the time to discuss
What about us

If it's what you need then I
Will accept the that you are moving on
But I refuse to believe that
You really permanently gone
So if you ever need to reach out to me
I'm never far
I'll always be around to
Revive the strings of your heart
And I truly believe that eventually
You'll come back around
To you and me

I WROTE THIS SONG

One moment in time
Your life walked into mine
And from that point on
I was completely changed
Because ever since your eyes
Looked up and met with mine
Nothing in my world
Has been the same

Reminiscing of the days
That we spent getting lost in the reveries
Love so fresh and pure my heart was yours
Never imagined it would all dissipate between you and me

And time keeps moving on
Days of us long gone
There's nothing I can do
So I wrote this song
To commemorate you and me
Keep us frozen
Locked in memory
So no matter how far we go
Locked in my heart you will always be

Reminiscing of the days
That we spent getting lost in the reveries
Love so fresh and pure my heart was yours
Never imagined it would all dissipate between you and me

And time keeps moving on
Days of us long gone
There's nothing I can do
So I wrote this song

WISDOM NUGGET 7

I believe you have to experience the full journey of love and loss. That includes bearing through the heartbreak of the ones who don't see you, and the ones who don't get you. The ones who don't reciprocate the passion and the energy you give, and the ones who simply don't care. It's tough but navigating through those who aren't for you to the one who is only for you makes it all worth it.

WISDOM NUGGET 8

If you find the person who can see deep into your soul with love, then you have found the one who can go the distance.

I'VE BEEN LOVING YOU SO LONG

So many days and nights
I thought it was you
The one who held my heartbeat
And I'm struggling with the realization that's it's not true
You're not the one for me
After all this time
My eyes were too blind to see
Is it all in vain
I want to give you happiness
But you cause me so much pain
It's crazy how the flame
Never stays ignited
Because we don't love the same
I've been loving you so long
That I can't see beyond us
And my heart can't move on
Even though I try hard to pretend
Deep down inside I know I'd make the choice
To do it all again
I can't deny the fact
That you're the one I can't let go of
My heart refuses to escape
The merry go round of love

YOU'LL NEVER KNOW

Hello again old love
Yes it's me
The one that you let go of
So easily
With no regard, you weren't thinking
Of how those tables turn
We meet again, it's been a long time
You're looking well
I'm doing fine
What's that look I'm seeing in your eyes
Let's stop right there

And I see your mind spinning
Trying to figure out why
My emotions are so cool
There's no longing in my eyes
I get no satisfaction
From showing no reaction
Because inside the truth is

You'll never know
The many sleepless nights
I stayed up late and cried
Feeling like my life was nothing
And without you, I would die
But time has been so healing
And growth has been unveiling
Sometimes it's so hard to let go

Of what we think we need
There's so much more to me
That you'll never know

Hold up my love
Don't walk away
Baby please
I'm begging you to stay
Come back to me; does that sound familiar
It should because it's a replay
Of all the countless times I called out for you
To give me love
And show that we were true
But all I got instead
Was broken promises and heartache
We can't go back
And undo our mistakes

And I see your mind spinning
Trying to figure out why
My emotions are so cool
There's no longing in my eyes
I get no satisfaction
From showing no reaction
Because inside the truth is

You'll never know
All of the days I wrecked myself trying to figure out why
I was never enough for you
So many ups and downs
You took me through
But time has been so healing
And growth has been unveiling
Sometimes it's so hard to let go
Of what we think we need

There's so much more to me
That you'll never know

The truth is being with you
Was nothing like I thought it would be
And I've come to the conclusion that
It was my love that made you unique
And I could go on and on
But it doesn't matter now anyway
You get no consolation
For the love you let slip away

FADED

I could have never imagined
A time in our lives where we'd come to this
It feels like such a bad dream
I always thought that we would withstand the challenges of life
But sometimes things aren't what they seem
I never thought much about it
But when I look back now
It was all so one sided
And all I can do now is move on

If I'm truly over it
Can you tell me why
The echoes of it all
Still make tears well up and leave my eyes

I don't know when it all got so complicated
Replaying everything back in my mind
The constant back and forth had me so jaded
And I guess I'll never truly know
Maybe I knew eventually we'd be separated
But I'm still fragile
Because I never pictured our love faded

And after everything we've been through
It's hard to believe that you and me
Were once so bonded and touchable
Now I only think of us as a memory
It hurt so much to walk away

We were so close
It's unfortunate to think of you now
From a distance as someone I used to know
But it takes two and you're not the only one
And I admit I played a part
In our connection becoming undone

If I'm truly over it
Can you tell me why
The echoes of it all
Still make tears well up and leave my eyes

I don't know when it all got so complicated
Replaying everything back in my mind
The constant back and forth had me so jaded
And I guess I'll never truly know
Maybe I knew eventually we'd be separated
But I'm still fragile
Because it hurts to know our friendship faded

It's so unfortunate
And it's crazy how our pride
Will cause us to miss every opportunity
We have to make things right
And I hold it all inside
Though I can't fake it as much as I try
Because I know I'll always
Endure the pain of our goodbye

WISDOM NUGGET 9

It's amazing how we don't realize that we can go through different versions of the same scenarios.

SUBCONSCIOUSLY

If you're ever wondering about me
And where it fell apart between us
You can think back to the last time it was supposed to be
You and I together as one
Instead you chose to walk away with no regard
Shattering our connection
I'll never understand how you had my love
And you don't even see what's obvious
I'm trying to figure out
When it all changed with us
Did you detach from transparency
Were you intimidated by vulnerability
Even if you never take the time to truly see me
And you don't value my affection
Let me send this message to you, subconsciously
Just in case
You're ever wondering about me

LETTING GO

I don't wanna talk about it
There's no more words to say
And even though I'm torn about it
I know I can't stay
So many restless nights
And countless tears I've cried
The thought of being without you
Has me broken inside
Yet still I realize

Even though I didn't want to believe
I'm past the point of being naive
I used to think you were my sanctuary
But it was all so temporary
And although I have to move on I know
That the hardest part is letting go

As I'm looking in your face
There's so much apathy in your eyes
They're revealing all the things
That your words are trying to hide
So if you feel that
You can't do right by me
Then I'll walk away
And let my heart be free
Because the truth is hard to deny

Even though I didn't want to believe

I'm past the point of being naive
I used to think you were my sanctuary
But it was all so temporary
And although I have to move on I know
That the hardest part is letting go

And after everything
It's a shame we couldn't get it right
But I don't wanna hurt, and I can't hope
We don't need to fight
Because it's so obvious
That the affection is gone
Now there's nothing left for us to do
But move on

BLIND

I guess hindsight is 20/20
Especially when it pertains to us
And now that I'm looking back on it all
All that I couldn't see is so obvious
I gave all of myself
Now we're obsolete
You had my whole heart
But you couldn't feel my beat

And if life is everything
You wanted it to be
Then tell me why
Are you reaching out to me

I was the one dedicated to you
It's a shame you couldn't see
But it's too late to come back
Because now I belong to me
You thought replacing me would be that easy
It's no surprise I'm on your mind
You had the best of my love
But you were blind

It's not that I
Expected you to be my savior
But I didn't think you'd do anything
That would break us
You could never endure all of my pain

All the time I was thinking we were fine
When in realty
Someone else was occupying your time

And if life is everything
You wanted it to be
Then tell me why
Are you reaching out to me

I was the one dedicated to you
It's a shame you couldn't see
But it's too late to come back
Because now I belong to me
You thought replacing me would be that easy
It's no surprise I'm on your mind
You had the best of my love
But you were blind

It hurt when I realized
You didn't reciprocate the love for me
And it was agony to accept the fact
That we weren't meant to be
Loving you left so many wounds
But it's a lesson learned
And although I truly wish you well
We're in the past and we can never return

LOVE SONG

Your words caress my mind like poetry
And I absorb everything you say to me
I am entranced at the things you do
You have gifted me the best parts of you
It's amazing how you've made me believe
In a romance I couldn't previously perceive

And ever since this thing with you began
I've been flying higher than I've ever been

Sounds like a love song
In my heart that goes on and on
Constantly replaying in my soul all night long
My heart shivers at the thought of you
And it feels marvelous
To be loved by someone that I love too

With you I am undisguised
My emotions are completely hypnotized
And I don't wanna rush the flow
Let's savor every moment and take it slow
Thoughts of us invade my mind
I wanna be with you all the time

And ever since this thing with you began
I've been flying higher than I've ever been

Sounds like a love song

In my heart that goes on and on
Constantly replaying in my soul all night long
My heart shivers at the thought of you
And it feels marvelous
To be loved by someone that I love too

An attachment so strong that even when we separate
I don't worry because we're worth the wait
So I'll sit here and dream of you
Until the next time we rendezvous
With you I feel like I'm whole from within
I'll think of you until I see your silhouette again

WISDOM NUGGET 10

My rule for my myself is this: If I have cried over it, hurt over it, stressed over it, prayed about it, and learned from it, I'm allowed to write about it. Period.

WRAPPED UP

It's an amazing feeling
To be able to finally breathe
And envision romance
In a way I couldn't previously see
Now that my heart is free and ready
To embrace someone new
I can finally admit to myself
The feelings I've been suppressing for you
And you always seem to find a way
To make me long to be wrapped up in your love
With tender moments of those mental kisses
And caresses of your verbal hugs
I know you feel the chemistry between us
How can you resist it
But for now, we're just a thought
That I will try to wish into existence

PART III

THIS ISN'T EVEN MY BEST LOOK

As much as I love writing, I went through a period where I didn't compose a poem, song, or journal entry. I call it the "dry period." It lasted about 4 years, from 2005 until 2009. Then, I realized that I had been neglecting a huge part of who I am.

At first, I was angry at myself for the way I stopped writing so abruptly, because it has always been a gift and a passion. It's my primary source of expression, and it allows me to be myself in a way that I feel I can be best understood. So, eventually, I started back writing everything that I could, and I haven't stopped since. It's crazy how we can lose focus on what's important to us when something else comes along that appears to be more appealing (or so it seems).

There was a long period in my life where I was not being my best self in any area. And despite certain circumstances beyond my control, I had no excuse. When you do not feel fully content with who you are, the insecurities can trickle down and affect every other aspect of your life. Technically, I was in what people like to call the "prime years". I should have been enjoying my best days, but I was doing anything but. And it was completely on me. Cockiness can cause us to overlook the warning signs, and we may think we are making the right choices. But if we are not careful, those choices can deter us from where we ultimately want to be. Admittedly, I lost sight of what I loved doing the most because I became consumed with trying to be what other people thought I should be. Consequently, I was trying to be someone I was not, which never works out well. I was in a long term relationship that I thought would lead to marriage, so I was completely focused on trying to be everything to my partner.

During this time, I was also trying to figure out what I wanted to do with my career, when my son was born in 2008. I don't even need to emphasize how life changing his birth was. Marriage, career success, and childbirth. For so many women, these are the three areas that we feel we have to check off in order to be whole. Even, if it means we aren't truly happy with the outcomes. I was certainly guilty of thinking that way.

I think all of these things are wonderful, as long as they are true reflections of a person's best self. At one point I was so focused on marriage, that I didn't realize I wanted to be committed to someone who didn't truly love me the way I deserved to be loved. If it becomes an obsession, it's not healthy. I have always been a hands on, full time mother, but I was so focused on working to survive, that my daily routine was almost robotic.

As a result, I did not give my son the best version of myself that he needed me to be. Luckily, he was young at the time, so I do not feel like he was greatly affected. Also, I was not as present as I should have been to my family and friends, and that caused some of my closest bonds to suffer.

Finally, I wanted to excel in a career field that hadn't been kind or fulfilling to me. I was going to work every day, but I was not giving it my all, which in turn caused me to be mediocre in my job roles. But for years I still chased after it. In fact, it was only after I sat down over the past year that I realized that I was very good at what I did; however, it wasn't where my passion was. And I certainly didn't want to be doing in for another five to ten years. I had to refocus and realign my priorities.

This meant I had to do some true introspection from the inside out. It was my responsibility to take accountability of my shortcomings. By doing so, I was able to get myself back on track to being fulfilled and succeeding in a way that I could be proud of. When everything came crashing down around me, I learned so many important lessons. At the time, it wasn't easy, and I was not happy. But the experience caused me to take a good and honest look at the path I was on, and whether it was mirroring who I really was and where I wanted to go. And I can't be mad about that.

I never expected my journey to be perfect, but I also never expected the many twists and turns I would encounter! We're so naive when we are younger; we expect to move through life unscathed. At least I did. Because I went through so much as a child, I thought that I had lived through the worst of everything, and everything going forward would be smooth. It was my arrogance that expected things to be great because it's what *I* felt I deserved. And that's how we can be at times, selfishly thinking that the world owes us something.

Obviously now, I know that's not how it works, but that's the ego of it all. I have been betrayed and hurt by people that I thought would always have my back. I have been dangerously depressed while putting on a smile to everyone around me. I have experienced the loss of love that I felt would be lasting. I have faced unexpected setbacks in my career that forced me to reevaluate where I was heading. And my life has unraveled when I thought it should have been the most stable. I used to think about which was worse: falling or getting back up. On one hand, the fall is usually unexpected, and when it happens it takes so much out of you. But getting back up requires the strength that has been taken away. Because of that, I have concluded that both scenarios include an equal amount of difficulty that must be overcome.

In my worst moments, I felt so defeated and alone. I admit I didn't always handle things the way I should. But that's what maturity, resilience and wisdom teaches us. We learn life is not about the absence of challenges and obstacles, as much as it's about how we handle what is put in front of us. So, I can say that sometimes, distractions serve a greater purpose. They can be just what we need to look inside, purge, and tune into what we really want out of life. And those are the best advantages that we can give to ourselves.

IT'S OCTOBER, AGAIN

When the leaves turn colors and they fall
And the season starts to change
That's when the silence gets so loud
And everything starts feeling strange
Because it sinks in that you're far away
But I long to have you near
I'd give anything if we could mend
Just to hold and have you here

It's not that I don't miss you
And wish for you any other time
But as the year counts down the memories
Settle in and overtake my mind
And I'm reminded that sometimes we don't get forever
Love is so special but it can end
And when the pain starts tugging at my heart
I know it's October again

As the sunny skies transform into gray
And my skin meets the cool air
I remember every vivid detail
Of sacred moments we used to share
That's when it all starts coming back to me
How much I ache to see your face
To feel the comfort of your loving arms
Embracing me into where I felt most safe

It's not that I don't miss you

And wish for you any other time
But as the year counts down the memories
Settle in and overtake my mind
And I'm reminded that sometimes we don't get forever
Love is so special but it can end
And when the pain starts tugging at my heart
I know it's October again

Most of the days I can get away
With holding my emotions deep within
Until time signals that the winds have changed
And the cycle of missing you all over begins

WISDOM NUGGET 11

Always be authentic with your intentions. Even if things don't turn out the way you hope, there is always comfort in being genuine with who you are.

WISDOM NUGGET 12

I have been knocked down more times than I can count. But I have learned how to get back up with wisdom and grace.

THE WAY CHRISTMAS SHOULD BE

Play my favorite Christmas song
On repeat for me
Let's snuggle by the fire
Next to the Christmas tree
As the scent of winter pine woods
Fill up in the air
I will wait around for reindeer all night
As long as you are there

Because us together for the holidays
Is all I need
Being with you makes everything complete
It's the way Christmas should be

As we shelter in from the cold
Let's steal a kiss below the mistletoe
As the children play outside
Making angels in the snow
Won't you come and spread the holly with me
And let good tidings lead the way
What means the most to me
Can't be brought on any sleigh

Because us together for the holidays
Is all I need
Being with you makes everything complete
It's the way Christmas should be

And as we gather to celebrate
Stars are dancing brightly up above
I ring those silver bells in memory
For the lost ones that we love
I'm so grateful that you're by my side
You are my Christmas dream come true
And every merry holiday I'll be alright
As long as I can spend it with you

HOW MANY MORE CHRISTMASES

It's the best time of the year
Where the days are filled with joy
And so much cheer
Everyone around me is embracing
Children count down the days
Eagerly anticipating
What's under the tree
I should be full of happiness too
But deep down inside
I'm so blue

I ask myself how many more Christmases
Will I be alone
It's hard to spend season after season
Celebrating on my own
I can't pretend that I
Don't long to be
In the presence of the one
Who truly loves me

I hear the sounds of couples laughter
And it seems that everyone else
Is getting their happily ever after
As I admire the glistening lights
I long to be wrapped up
And held tight
By the one I adore
I wonder if I will ever again have the chance

To feel the warmth
Of a beautiful holiday romance

I ask myself how many more Christmases
Will I be alone
It's hard to spend season after season
On my own
I can't pretend that I
Don't long to be
In the presence of the one
Who truly loves me

Even though right now it's hard to see
I still believe there is
Some December magic left for me
So I hope that this time next year
Love will have found me
And it will forever be near

WISDOM NUGGET 13

Our thoughts can be both a blessing and a curse. It's my thoughts that have afforded me with the gift of creative transparency. However, those same thoughts were a great source of pain, insecurity, doubt, and fear. Over time, I have learned how to use my experiences and my mind as a way of healing to move forward and possibly touch others in the process.

WISDOM NUGGET 14

One of the best things about writing for me has been the ability to see myself fully. I get to see and compare my emotions and thoughts from my younger self to who I am now. There are some similarities, but there are also some vast differences. What's most fascinating is that I get a glimpse of the things that I have healed from and moved past, as well as the areas where I still struggle.

WILL I (AGAIN)

Sometimes this life
Can be so lonely
I can't help but wonder
If I'm the only
One who struggles to calm
Those overwhelming things
That rise to the surface
When uncertainty brings
Those inklings of doubt
And I'm left contemplating
How to sort it all out

Will I ever feel the assurance
Of normalcy again
Will the holes in my heart
Ever completely mend
And I try to find the strength
To heal from deep within
But what if I never
Feel stable again

When my mind can't seem
To escape the dejected place
And despite my best efforts
I still can't find a space
Where sanctuary can come
And pull me back in
To where there is balance

So I can begin
To quiet the voice inside
From trying to convince me
That in the shadows is where I should hide

Will I ever feel the assurance
Of normalcy again
Will the holes in my heart
Ever completely mend
And I try to find the strength
To heal from deep within
But what if I never
Feel worthy again

When my worst days
Seem to be never ending
And the clouds of desolation
Are persistent and unrelenting
I still realize this life
Is calling for me
To look beyond the darkness
Into the light I can see

FALL AWAY

When everything around you feels so broken
Don't you forget to breathe
And if the situation feels impossible
Remember all you have to do is believe
That you can make it through
To the other side of the rain
If you just keep moving steadily
And let your heart guide you through the pain
If you hold on you will survive
To see the resolution of brighter days
Life storms are tough but they always dissipate
And eventually all of the anguish will fall away

WISDOM NUGGET 15

If your way of determining my value and worth is by checking off the proverbial boxes based on who you think I should be, you won't get very far with me. I don't operate inside of boxes. In fact, I make it a point to think (and live) outside of them.

INVISIBLE

When you're feeling lost
And deep in despair
If you are convinced
That nobody cares
When you find it hard
To make it through the days
But solace still seems
To be so far away

When your heart is not at ease
And your soul can't find peace
Even if you feel alone
You can prevail on your own

Don't you be discouraged
I'm always here for you
Regardless of where you are
Or what you're going through
When it seems that life is far from perfect
And the road gets difficult
This a confirmation that you always have a friend
So you never feel invisible

In those trying times
That you don't understand
Why the world is closing in
Yet no one offers you a hand
If you're searching for a remedy

When it seems like you are falling down
And when you reach for empathy
There is no one around

When your heart is not at ease
And your soul can't find peace
Even if you feel alone
You can prevail on your own

Don't you be discouraged
I'm always here for you
Regardless of where you are
Or what you're going through
When it seems that life is far from perfect
And the road gets difficult
This a confirmation that you always have a friend
So you never feel invisible

When you're losing hope
Let faith be your shelter
And lean on love for the promise
That everything will get better

WISDOM NUGGET 16

We cannot afford to fill up others at the expense of depleting ourselves.

WISDOM NUGGET 17

Doing what's best for you won't always be liked or understood by others. Those are the times that you should do it without hesitation.

PART IV

A MILLION SMALL STEPS

"To get from the girl I was to the woman I am now took a million small steps..." I remember writing this statement years ago with confidence. At the time I felt it was so poignant and so real; but even then, I didn't fully understand the meaning of what I was saying. Isn't that interesting how we can iterate something, without knowing the full magnitude? I am still very much a work in progress, and I still have so much to learn. There are areas of my life that I feel that I have mastered the art of learning how to deal, while in other areas I am still working to do better. In the summer of 2018, it hit one of the lowest points in my life mentally, physically, and emotionally. There was one day in particular that caused me to assess everything in its entirety. I was driving home from work, and I had so many different emotions at once. I had been feeling off balance for a while, but on this day, I couldn't even calm down enough to get a handle on myself. This was a different type of feeling. It was unfamiliar, and it was very scary because I was afraid, I was going to have an accident because I couldn't snap out of it to drive home safely. I realized then that I needed some help to sort out everything I was feeling because I would no longer do it by myself. I was exhausted in every way, and I felt I was nearing my breaking point. It was an accumulation of everything that had taken place over the prior years, and it had reached a plateau. I knew that my son deserved the best of me, and I deserved it as well. So, I made the decision to start therapy. It was long overdue, and it was very necessary. It turned out to be a turning point for me in the best way. Trying to make sense of everything that is going on your head and your heart can be very difficult, especially when you don't feel like you have support. Growing up as a Christian, therapy was looked at as being a bit taboo. Like so many others, I was taught that the only source of healing was God and prayer. And for so long I was never fully able to share how I was feeling inside out of fear that I would be judged. I can remember hearing my elders having conversations about spirituality and therapy and them saying that the two didn't go together. Those words stuck with me, and for long I thought that was the truth. I am very much a believer, and my faith has seen me through some of my darkest days, as well as my greatest challenges. But when you are hurt, and in pain you have to be able to rely on something more. Healing comes from admission and truth. It wasn't until I got older that I realized that there was no shame in being able to open up and share my feelings to someone, especially if they can help with the restoration. When I sat down with my therapist for our first session, she asked me why I was meeting with her. I couldn't hold it in any longer, and I just broke down. I think I was because I had so many things what were boiling up to the surface because they were never properly addressed. I also felt that it was the first time that someone was concerned with my well-being and how I was doing from a unbiased point of view. That makes a huge difference. Being able to sort through all my high and low points has been the best form of self-care. It was so healing, and eye opening because there were so many things that we discussed in a way that I hadn't been open to before. I was able to be real with myself and address my mess. But I was also able to remove the weights off my shoulders that hadn't been placed there by me. And I was able to shed a lot of old skin. During one session, my therapist pointed out that even though our time is supposed to be all about me, I still made it a point to be thoughtful of others. Even she was saying it as a positive compliment, it highlighted something that has been both a strength and an Achilles heel for me. And that is me being considerate to others, even when it's a distraction from me focusing on myself. It brought back all the many times I had stayed loyal to people that had hurt me. And I had to acknowledge that I was still allowing people to have access to me, even though they were not deserving. That's when I realized I had to establish some major boundaries in my life. The first step was forgiving myself for all of the times I allowed someone's disrespect to overshadow my value. I could no longer afford to be meek. I had to stand in my truth and be firm, regardless of what anyone thought about it. Of course, when you reach that stage in your life, it means that certain things and people will no longer be a part of it, and I was okay with that. At this moment, I get to dictate what my life looks like, how I get to live it, and who gets to come along for the journey.

So, what does the journey of "a million small steps" mean to me right now? It means so many things. It's being able to fully embrace my past with no shame or regret. It's not being embarrassed to admit that I am not perfect. It's having the courage to start over, because I know rather than starting from scratch I am starting from experience and wisdom. I understand now that backtracking doesn't have to be a negative thing, and that it can be necessary. I am proud of my ability to express myself.

To me, there is nothing worse than feeling stifled, and being made to think that speaking your mind in any situation is wrong or unattractive. It is never wise to compare yourself to anyone, but I used to do it anyway. And when I compared myself to others, I used to think that I was not truly living and that my life was dull. When I truly began to grasp my purpose and my calling, I understood why my life did not look like anyone else's. There is always a method to the madness, and a process to the progress. I have learned to keep moving and have faith, even in the roughest moments.

I can attest to being saved by grace when I struggling to find my way out of the fire. I can also say that's it's a miracle that I didn't go completely over the edge, even in those times where I didn't think I could take it all anymore. Moving through my journey, this is what I have learned: You can love genuinely with all your heart, and still be hurt. You can think more of people than they think of you. You can do everything the right way, and still come up short. You can plan meticulously, and still be blindsided by the unforeseen. You can stray, and you will make mistakes. And yet, you can still come out better than you could have ever imagined.

Life is anything but predictable. I can confidently say that no matter what is thrown at me, I will be okay through it all. I stand on that without a doubt because I have my own rear view lens to prove it. And to anyone who may be experiencing the complexities of life and trying to figure out where they fit (trying to make sense of it all), please know this: you are me, and I am you.

WISDOM NUGGET 18

How much time do we spend denying our true selves? Ignoring what lies in the depth of our hearts is never beneficial, because what is true will always resurface and demand to be seen.

ISOLATION

Is it habitual for me to be discreet
To keep the parts unseen
That tend to be most vulnerable to deceit
There's so much I want to unveil
But apprehension keeps me torn
When I think of what the consequences could entail
So here I stand so eager to release
Because I know that it's the only way
To be completely at peace
Although I'm tempted to act without hesitation
Sometimes it's easier
To stay hidden safely in isolation

WISDOM NUGGET 19

When I was deciding on how to put this book together, initially I thought of lumping all the similar songs and poems into the same category. But then, I took an honest reflection of my life, and what a roller-coaster it has been. In doing so, I realized that the purpose was to tell the complete story. So, it seemed logical for me to tell that story as the realistic whirlwind, up and down journey that it has been and I think it works.

ANYTHING

I would give anything
If I could
Reveal the intricate parts of me
Without being misunderstood
If I could just communicate
All of the things I can't say modestly
Without fear of judgment
Or the risk of dishonesty

If I believed that I could be
Transparent and unapologetically me
That would mean everything
And I would give anything

Is it even possible
For me to truly exist in
The space of my surroundings
Without having to give in
To a world that keeps me muted
And I am caught in between
But I long to be released to
Where I can be completely seen

If I believed that I could be
Transparent and unapologetically me
That would mean everything
And I would give anything

I guess it's true
That I've become immune
To all the ways that life
Can make me feel subdued
And when the weight becomes
Too much to bear
Inside I hope for someone to see
That I am here
Because that would mean everything
And I would give anything

WISDOM NUGGET 20

Sometimes, even I'm bewildered at how I'm still standing despite everything I've been through. Obstacles and hard times can birth incredible testimonies if we are brave enough to get to the other side of the pain.

WISDOM NUGGET 21

Now I can breathe. The big exhale.

MY LIFE, SO FAR

I used to think that I could see
The perfect image of my life
And what it would turn out to be
But now that I am older I know
The road can be unpredictable
There's been so many highs and lows
Although I've handled so many twists and turns
Still I realize
There's still so much for me to learn

When I take it all in
It reads like an imperfect memoir
But I'm thankful for every step in the journey
Of my life so far
So I praise every victory
And embrace every scar
Because I recognize it was necessary to the story
Of my life so far

I've took my share of losses and made mistakes
And I have often wondered
How many disappointments one heart could take
Still I've pressed on through it all
Because I know I have a guiding grace
There to catch me if I fall
It's not always easy but it's up to me
To pick up the broken pieces
And set myself free

When I take it all in
It reads like an imperfect memoir
But I'm thankful for every step in the journey
Of my life so far
So I praise every victory
And embrace every scar
Because I recognize it was necessary to the story
Of my life so far

There's a part of me that will always conceal
The areas of my heart
That will never completely heal
But I prevail because my faith has kept me warm
It carried me in my public battles
And brought me through my private storms
And I believe
I was pulled back from the edge so generously
Because I have a guiding grace looking out for me

"Now you're dressed in a new wardrobe. Every item of your new way of life is custom-made by the Creator, with his label on it. All the old fashions are now obsolete."

Colossians 3:10 (The Message)

A LITTLE CONTEXT BEHIND MY WORK

Everything that I write has a meaning, and it tells a story. They are based on exact memories with the people involved. The pieces about myself, my mother, or my son I feel are obvious. They speak for themselves (as they should). However, anything that pertains to my relationships are a bit more discrete. For many reasons, I choose to keep those specifics more private. But I did want to share some details surrounding the inspirations (without giving too much away). I realize that reading a song may be a little difficult when there is no music. For me, the melodies are always in my head. For anyone else, it may be more sensible to read all the pieces as poems, even the songs.

Through The Clouds

My mother was huge part of my life. Her death left a hole in my heart that has never completely healed. And it never will. She is one of the main inspirations behind everything I do. This song was a way for me to memorialize her, but more than that it was one of the many ways I talk to her.

A Field of Strawberries for Traci

This poem was based on a fun detail about my mother. When I was growing up, everybody had a "theme" that they decorated their house around. For my mother, it was strawberries. I laugh when I think about it now, but back then it was so annoying because she was obsessed with getting her hands on any type of strawberry decor she could find. It was so bad, that even her friends and family would buy her things.

Luckily, she only decorated the kitchen in strawberries. I wasn't really a fan, but there was one item in particular that I loved. It was a framed picture of a bowl of strawberries, and it was stunning to look at because it was so realistic. It had such a lasting effect, and of course anytime I see a strawberry I think of her. They are beautiful, just like she was. And even though she's no longer here, I like to imagine her surrounded by strawberries.

Reminisce

When I was growing up, I used to count the days until I was older. I thought it was going to be the greatest thing ever. Of course, the adults around me would always say to enjoy being young while I could, because I would wish for those days again when they were gone. Once I became an adult, I understood everything they were saying. It's the same thing that I reiterate to my sisters, and anyone younger than me. This song was heavily inspired by my cousin Meoshi (or as I call her, Meme). Our fathers are brothers, making us first cousins. I am about a year older than her, and like my two male cousins on my mother's side, we have also been close since we were kids. We spent so much time together, and I can recall so many days and nights where we anticipated being able to do whatever we wanted once we were considered to be of age. Being in the trenches of it all now is quite a whirlwind. Adulthood has its advantages; however, I miss those simple days I spent in my room without a care.

4:01 (Jayden's Song)

A song dedicated to my favorite person. When I was with Jayden's father, I knew I wanted to be a mother. Even when we weren't trying, I hoped to have a baby someday. I took so many pregnancy tests throughout our relationship, hoping they were positive. One day, after being disappointed by yet another negative result, he told me something foreshadowing. He said that when I did become pregnant, I wouldn't suspect it, because we'd had so many false alarms. And he was right. When I was really pregnant, despite having so many symptoms, I brushed them off. I think I didn't want to get my hopes up to be disappointed yet again, so I didn't allow myself to think beyond the moment. But deep down I knew something was different with my body. So, the morning of my doctor's appointment, I said a prayer in the waiting room for my unborn child. Shortly after, my pregnancy was confirmed by my doctor. I was shocked, and so happy. I immediately fell in love with him, and he has been a delight ever since.

A Breath of Fresh Air for Demond

While I was editing my book to get it finalized, he passed away suddenly. This person who meant the word to me for so long was...gone. Just like that. We experienced so many phases of life during our journey of knowing one another. And it was not always pretty, but over time we were able to get to this amazing place of understanding and acceptance. At one point we had a romantic relationship. And even after it ended, we remained in each other's lives. What eventually developed was a genuine friendship that was better than I could have asked for.

One of the things that bonded us when we were younger was pain. I was always better at being expressive, but he used to have so many walls up. As we got to know each more and learned to trust, those walls slowly came down. I have not fully accepted him not being here. I take things day by day. It is 20 years of love, friendship, and unforgettable memories.

There are so many things connected to our journey, that at times I want to seclude myself so that I don't have these constant reminders. Everything is a trigger because the time span that included him my life is so huge. And that is what is crushing. He saw my heart, and he dared to understand my soul. My comfort is the fact that there were never any words left unspoken. There was always full transparency where our feelings were involved. At times, I know that drove him crazy, but I also know he appreciated the honestly. I knew that that he was never far, but we did not talk all the time. That did not bother me, because I knew that eventually we would lay eyes on each other. Knowing that will not happen anymore hurts my soul. I will never get over the loss. I will never be okay with it. The empty spot in my heart can be overwhelming at times, and the ache is never ending. But he was one of the most important parts of my life, and I will forever be grateful that our paths crossed.

There are a good number of written pieces in this book that detailed our relationship. (Of course, I will not call them out). We both shared a love of reading, and he was also an amazing writer, so I was looking forward to his feedback once he read my book. I know that would have given his opinion whether I asked for it or not. And he would have never admitted it, but he would have been curious to know which pieces were about him. I suppose now he knows without question. He used to tell me that I was his breath of fresh air. And with him, I knew I could breathe. So, I guess we're even. See you later, D.

Crash Into You

Some people stay with you forever. No matter what happens, or how much time passes they always remain in your heart. And you may not know how or when, but them coming back into your life again (in some capacity) is inevitable. They are a recurrence in your life, but that doesn't mean they will stay for long. Even if deep down you want them to.

Without You

This was the first song I ever wrote. I was 19, and I had been preparing myself to write for years. But every time I would get an idea, I could never finish it. But on this particular night I had finally built up the nerve, so I sat down and decided I wouldn't stop until I had a completed piece of work. After about an hour, this song was the result. At the time, I was still dealing with a lot of emotions regarding someone I loved. There was a lot of back and forth between us, and we just could not figure out a way to make it stick (because, well we were young adults). I wanted the song to be perfect, and I was so selective with my words. I was so happy when I had finished, and at the time I thought I had really done something. Reading it now, I realize how melodramatic it is. It's just so depressing and "woe is me". But at the time, it incorporated everything I was going through and how I felt. Plus, it started a writing journey for me, and for that I will always be proud of it.

Illusion (A Poem)

Relationships that are inconsistent can be so perplexing. The uncertainty can cause you to question if what you're experiencing is even real, or if it's more of a Snuffaluffgus love. (I couldn't help myself with this reference). But at least I can laugh about it now.

Dismissed

I'd had enough. I had turned myself inside out, and I was just over it all. There was nothing else to do, feel, or want. All that was left was goodbye. To be fair, we both had a lot of growing up to do at the time. But I was still pissed and over it.

All Over Again

Have you ever been moving along in your life at a steady pace, then you come face to face with the one person who can stop you in your tracks? This was that. And I knew better, because I had been down this road before, and it didn't end well. And this was someone who was hard to get over. To the point where I would have to start the process of getting over him from scratch and erase all the progress I had made previously each time I backtracked. I hit that relationship wall constantly until I got tired. But it took a very long time.

Suddenly

Sometimes, when you aren't looking, a person enters your life, and they take you by surprise. Even when you try to ignore the feeling, you can't get away from it. Love that comes out of nowhere, is such a nice change of pace. It can be so wonderful, even if it's only for a moment.

Shatter

There are times in our relationships where we can sense the end is near, and we may even be okay with it depending on the situation. But then, there are those moments that we don't ever see coming. With this relationship, at the time I thought we were going to be end game. I thought I was with my person. So, when things came to a sudden halt, I was completely blindsided. And it knocked the wind out of me. I couldn't comprehend what had happened. At the time it seemed like it was the end of the world, and I would never get over it. Even though it's still crazy to think about, I realize everything that happened was for the best.

You

How many ways can you write about love, heartbreak, and everything in between? Well, a lot. There are many to convey your emotions, and I wrote every time the feeling came to me. So, here's *another* song about my relationship with *that* guy. Hmmm…

Lingering

How hard it is when your mind wants to move on, but your heart won't allow it.

Healing

So, this song is centered around restlessness, and the amount of energy that we often give to pain before everything starts to feel better. If I think back to every sleepiness night that I stayed up agonizing over a relationship in some way, it would probably add up to years (which is kind of sad). And I was up late one night, thinking about someone (once again), and I decided to capture my thoughts. A funny tidbit: this was one of those songs for me, that took a bit longer to write. I would start it, and then get blocked after a certain point. When I finished the second verse, I was so irritated that I didn't want to add a third verse to it and I didn't. So, anyone who reads it might be thinking that it's incomplete. In a way it is, but I left it that way on purpose. To me, it works.

One More Time

How many times did I say I was done? And it was true until I heard his voice. How many times did I claim that the door to reconciliation was closed, when it was really cracked? My heart paid the price every time.

The Unchosen

I was pretty angry when I wrote this poem. But I think it translates as sadness. Life can be unpredictable and unfair. And even though I have no regrets, and I realize that everything happens for a reason, the human side of me still gets a little weary at times. Being the understanding person, the bigger person, the mature person constantly can be so discouraging. Not to mention draining.

Until We Meet Again

A favorite memory with my favorite connection. The climax. We are bonded together through time, indefinitely. So grateful to be a part of the kismet.

What About Us

It was going so well, and I wanted us to continue to move forward. But I was so overzealous that I didn't allow the relationship to progress as naturally as it should have. Too much over thinking and overreaction stopped everything, and it was only fair. I was wrong, and I learned a tough lesson. I'm not much of a "what if" person, but I do ponder what we could have been, if only….

I Wrote This Song

I was thinking about an old love. It was great, and it was fun. I wish it would have lasted longer, but we were unaware, and we were young.

I've Been Loving You So Long

A repetitive moment. Nothing new under the moonlight. Just another night spent thinking about the nuances of love. It's crazy how we're the same, yet we are so different….

You'll Never Know

For the most part, I think we are aware of how we treat others. However, I do think we can be unaware of the severity of how someone can be affected when we don't treat them well. We can be oblivious to the amount of pain we cause, and the recovery process a person has to endure. As I was standing in front of this person, he was baffled by my indifferent demeanor. But it's only because he didn't fully understand what it took for me to get to that point.

Faded

I wrote this with a dual meaning. It represents the ending of a relationship, as well as a couple of friendships that meant so much to me. Even if we don't like it, sometimes, we reach the end of the line with people in all areas of our life. But it still hurts like hell.

Subconsciously

Based off an actual conversation, just with slightly different wording. But it's all the same meaning.

Letting Go

The moment of no return. The penultimate. The place between pain, and healing. More importantly, the realization that it's time to move forward without turning back.

Blind

Have you ever been so surprised to hear from someone that when they call, you just stare at your phone out of disbelief? Or perhaps, you're just in awe of the audacity. Yeah, that's more like it. But that conversation felt good because I was good. I was finally in a better frame of mind and thought, and there's was nothing that was going to change it. I never take pleasure in anyone's misery or unhappiness. However, I will always delight in the person that I am. And whether people figure that out about me sooner or later is up to them.

Love Song

An ode to love in its purest form: sensual, incomparable, and discrete.

Wrapped Up

It happens suddenly. After the long (and sometimes seemingly never ending) saga of heartbreak and disappointment, you come out of hiding. And once again, your heart is free and open to the opportunity of what can be in love. And just like that, you are in a new space.

It's October, Again

Hands down, the season I love the most is fall. And my favorite month of the year is October. To me, October represents transition and change. It's beautiful and mysterious at the same time. This is the one song that wasn't necessarily written with a particular person in mind, because in truth it can pertain to more than one person depending on the year. For me, it ultimately represents how we can long for whatever we feel is missing from our lives. So, I suppose "October" is a metaphor.

The Way Christmas Should Be

It's no secret that I love Christmas. No matter what's going on in my life, the holiday season always puts me in a great mood. Decorating, beautiful scenery, my favorite scents, family time, great food, festive music, cheesy Hallmark movies, and I could go on and on. It's truly the best. Some of my favorite songs are the ones about the holidays. I've always wanted to write a fun Christmas song, and this one makes me happy.

How Many More Christmases

Of course, I wouldn't be me if I didn't write a sappy, brooding song about the holidays. In all seriousness, Christmas is amazing, but it can also feel very lonely. I've definitely felt it, and I know many others have as well.

Will I (Again)

Depression in its most challenging form. So many people, including myself have struggled with not being okay at some point in life. It's still a very touchy subject to discuss for so many. And I think it's because depression can stifle you so much to the point where you are ashamed. It's hard to explain your feelings and thoughts, especially when you don't know why you are having them. The process of climbing out of the darkness is different for so many people. For me personally, it took self-reflection, acceptance, strength, therapy, and the strong will to want to survive. And I still have my down days. We all go through so much, and you really never know what's going on with the person beside you.

Fall Away

I think it's good to lift up others when have the opportunity. We can never have too many words of encouragement. You never know how they may stick with someone.

Invisible

At times, I have felt what I like to call "invisible syndrome." There are days when I think to myself, "I am here, right?" There are times where I don't feel seen, and it can be hard. As I have gotten older, I have learned to not take it so personally. Life can deal a series of blows that can cause you to feel defeated. But it does get better. I wrote this song for myself as much as I wrote it for others. I like to think of the words as an angel on my shoulders.

Isolation

I've always considered myself to be quite an introvert and can seem to be a bit of an oxymoron when it comes to writing. I love expression; however, I also love keeping things to myself. At times, it feels like I'm literally pulling myself in two opposite directions. The word "isolation" took on many forms over the past year, and I wrote this song during the Covid-19 pandemic. To me, it's symbolic because it truly represents both sides of me. There is the part of me that purposely shelters herself as a defense mechanism, and the other part that releases it all to be free.

Anything

I never cared about fitting in. It wasn't my thing. In fact, I knew at a young age that I moved differently, and I preferred it that way. But genuine connection is something that I think that we all wish for. We are not put on this earth to be alone. Companionship and acceptance from that one and only person is the best feeling. It doesn't matter how much we say we don't want it or need it, we do. It's very vital.

My Life, So Far

Such an incredible piece for me to complete. I was really trying to incorporate everything about my life into a song, which was not easy. I wanted it to be inspirational and uplifting. But I also wanted to be honest. My purpose was to convey that even with everything that has happened up to this point in my life, here I am. I'm not perfect, my life is not perfect, and I am figuring it all out like most people. I embrace what is behind me. But I'm so blessed and so excited about what is ahead.

I knew that certain words would be reoccurring throughout my book due to the content. Initially, I thought the most used word would be love. But I think the most used word is memory. I'm very big on words (obviously), and I love to find different synonyms and connotations as a way to say something. But sometimes, it just wasn't possible. It's fitting that *memory* is one of my most used phrases. After all, it's the memories that we hold onto because ultimately, it's all we are left with. Memories make us laugh, cry, and reflect. But more than that, they are a reminder that something significant in our life happened. Good or bad, the moments are eternally timestamped. And for that I am filled with gratitude.

www.ingramcontent.com/pod-product-compliance
Lightning Source LLC
Chambersburg PA
CBHW072036110526
44592CB00012B/1440